IT'S ALL ABOUT LOVE

PRINCE
ALADE MATT

2022

Subtitle

Deep guideline in a relationship lead to marriage

DESCRIPTION

The (IT'S ALL ABOUT LOVE) is a book dedicated to my ex, it's been my very long time experience throughout the relationship with my ex, it's just a guidelines in a relationship

Chapter 1:- Beauty

You area beautiful person that deserves to be happy so stop crying. The person who hurt you did not know how amazing you are. They don't know what they're missing. Don't give up yet. Everything will fall into place. You will find the person who deserves you and sees the best in you.

Chapter 2:- Romantic

When you love someone, it''s nothing. When someone loves you, it''s something. When u luv someone & they luv you back, it''s everything i love my eyes when u look into them; I luv my name when u say it; I luv my heart when u luv it; I love my life when you are in it.

Chapter 3:- Attitude

One passion can only be cured by another..a misplaced love by a greater love, wrong behavior by right behavior that makes provisions for the desire underlying the wrongdoing, recognizes the conscious or unconscious needs that seek fulfillment and either offers them legitimate satisfaction or transfers them to something compatible with the person's calling.

Chapter 4 :- Caring

You can be the most beautiful person in the world and everybody sees light and rainbows when they look at you, but if you yourself don't know it, all of that doesn't even matter. Every second that you spend on doubting your worth, every moment that you use to criticize yourself; is a second of your life wasted, is a moment of your life thrown away. It's not like you have forever, so don't waste any of your seconds, don't throw even one of your moments away.

Chapter 5:- complicated love

You Are My Pillar Of Strength Who Has Always Guided Me Through The Best And The Worst. You Are The One Who Stopped Me From Pulling Down The Blinds When The Windows Of The Best Opportunities Opened. Thanks For Being A Part Of My Like. It Could Not Have Been Better Than This.

Chapter 6:- Love Advice <i>

When life becomes too complicated and we feel overwhelmed, it's often useful just to stand back and remind ourselves of our overall purpose, our overall goal. When faced with a feeling of stagnation and confusion, it may be helpful to take an hour, an afternoon, or even several days to simply reflect on what it is that will truly bring us happiness, and then reset our priorities on the basis of that. This can put our life back in proper context, allow a fresh perspective, and enable us to see which direction to take.

Chapter 7:- Love Advice <ii>

To have regret is to be disappointed with yourself and your choices. Those who are wise, see their life like stepping stones across a great river. Everyone misses a stone from time to time. No one can cross the river without getting wet. Success is measured by your arrival on the other side, not on how muddy your shoes are. Regrets are only felt by those who do not understand life's purpose. They become so disillusioned that they stand still in the river and do not take the next leap.

Chapter 8:- Love Advice <iii>

The best relationship is when we can act like lovers and bestfriend. It's when you have more playful moments then serious moments. It's when you can joke around, have unexpected hugs, and random kisses.It's when we give each other that specific stare and just smile. It's when you'll stay up all night just to settle your arguments and problem. It's when you can completely act yourself and they can still love you for who you are.

Chapter 9:- Distance Love <i>

A Long-distance Relationship Is No Different From A Proximal Relationship In That They Both Require A Great Deal Of Work, Excellent Communication, Patience, Sacrifice And Understanding. But You Will Have To Work Extra Hard To Maintain The Communication And To Stay Focused Enough To Not Let Your Daily Life Interfere With Your Desire To Be With The Other Person. Don't Forget Them Or You Can Forget The Relationship And It Will All Be Over.

Chapter 10:- Distance Love <ii>

When Talking To Your Partner, Take Note Of Things They Enjoy The Most (hobbies, Day-to-day Activities, Etc.), And Do A Little Research On It So You Have More To Do When You See Them Next. For Example: If Your Partner Likes To dance, Find The Location Of Different Clubs Where You Will See Them Next. If You Don't Know How To dance, Take Lessons And You Will Impress Them By Your Willingness To Make An Effort On Their Behalf.

Chapter 11:- Love Proverb

Love Me When I Least Deserve It, Because That's When I Really Need It.

Fear less, hope more, eat less, chew more, whine less, breathe more, talk less, say more, love more, and all good things will be yours.

In order to really love someone, you must love him as though he was going to die tomorrow.

You Can Give Without Loving, But You Can't Love Without Giving.

Chapter 12:- Marriage Love <i>

We have a long way to go to being the perfect couple, we certainly don't live the fairy tale marriage, he doesn't shower me with rose petals and fly me to Paris on weekends but when I get my hair cut, he notices. When I dress up to go out at night, he compliments me. When I cry, he wipes my tears. When I feel lonely, he makes me feel loved. And who needs Paris, when you can get a hug?

Chapter 13:- Marriage Love <ii>

The point of marriage is not to create a quick commonality by tearing down all boundaries; on the contrary, a good marriage is one in which each partner appoints the other to be the guardian of his solitude, and thus they show each other the greatest possible trust. A merging of two people is an impossibility, and where it seems to exist, it is a hemming-in, a mutual consent that robs one party or both parties of their fullest freedom and development. But once the realization is accepted that even between the closest people infinite distances exist, a marvelous living side-by-side can grow up for them, if they succeed in loving the expanse between them, which gives them the possibility of always seeing each other as a whole and before an immense sky.

Chapter 14:- Show Your Love <i>

I will Try to win, even if am Losing.I will Try to have Hope, even if there is None.I will Try always to Smile, even if I m Crying.I will Try to Sing, even if my Voice is dying.Copyright lovelysms.comI will Try to be Positive , even if I m surrounded in Negatives.I will Try to reach for the Heaven, even if I m in Hell.I will Try to Love , even if I have a Broken Heart. Love you always Darling.

Chapter 15:- Show Your Love <ii>

If I got a dime for every time I thought about how deeply I love you, I would have been the world's richest man by now. But I know for a fact that my love for you is far more valuable than any riches life could possibly offer. I love you.

I Was a Smoker!!!Once I Read: “Smoking Is Injurious To Health”I QUIT Smoking.I Used To Drink Wine I Read: “WINE is Bad For Health”I Left Drinking.I LOVE Someone

Once I Read: “Love is an illusion”You Know What I Did?I Left “Reading”!

love
you

love, peace, and joy

FROM THE FITZGERALDS

www.ingramcontent.com/pod-product-compliance
Lightning Source LLC
LaVergne TN
LVHW020547160826
845677LV00015B/4241